Bizarre Behaviour

AF059795

BookLife RAPID Readers

IN ANCIENT ROME

All rights reserved.
Printed in India.

A catalogue record for this book is available from the British Library.

ISBN: 978-1-80505-604-1

Written by:
Shalini Vallepur
Adapted by:
Noah Leatherland
Edited by:
Elise Carraway
Designed by:
Jasmine Pointer

©2024
BookLife Publishing Ltd.
King's Lynn, Norfolk
PE30 4LS, UK

All facts, statistics, web addresses and URLs in this book were verified as valid and accurate at time of writing. No responsibility for any changes to external websites or references can be accepted by either the author or publisher.

AN INTRODUCTION TO BOOKLIFE RAPID READERS...

Packed full of gripping topics and twisted tales, BookLife Rapid Readers are perfect for older children looking to propel their reading up to top speed. With three levels based on our planet's fastest animals, children will be able to find the perfect point from which to accelerate their reading journey. From the spooky to the silly, these roaring reads will turn every child at every reading level into a prolific page-turner!

CHEETAH

The fastest animals on land, cheetahs will be taking their first strides as they race to top speed.

MARLIN

The fastest animals under water, marlins will be blasting through their journey.

FALCON

The fastest animals in the air, falcons will be flying at top speed as they tear through the skies.

Photo Credits

Images are courtesy of Shutterstock.com. With thanks to Getty Images, Thinkstock Photo and iStockphoto.
COVER & RECURRING – JORDEN MARBLE, luckyraccoon, ONYXprj, PCH.Vector. 4–5 – Vlas Telino studio, Sidhe. 6–7 – Kraft74, Morphart Creation, ONYXprj. 8–9 – AlexAnton, Kuhn, Public domain, via Wikimedia Commons. 10–11 – Matankic, CC BY-SA 4.0 <https://creativecommons.org/licenses/by-sa/4.0>, via Wikimedia Commons, ZenitX. 12–13 – BEAUTY STUDIO, autbmoore, Kovaleva_Ka, Dmitriy Kazitsyn, baldezh, Leestudio. 14–15 – domnitsky, zevana, Nick N A, xpixel. 16–17 – LouieLea, Evannovostro. 18–19 – Koca Vehbi, fotopanorama360, Natalllenka.m, WinWin artlab. 20–21 – SergeyKlopotov, Yair Haklai, CC BY-SA 4.0 <https://creativecommons.org/licenses/by-sa/4.0>, via Wikimedia Commons. 22–23 – WH_Pics, Laurent Renault. 24–25 – isawnyu, CC BY 2.0 <https://creativecommons.org/licenses/by/2.0>, via Wikimedia Commons, Tomasz Guzowski. 26–27 – Geza Farkas, Carole Raddato from FRANKFURT, Germany, CC BY-SA 2.0 <https://creativecommons.org/licenses/by-sa/2.0>, via Wikimedia Commons. 28–29 – staff.4j.lane.edu, Public domain, via Wikimedia Commons, Eivaisla, Akarawut, Dora Zett, Billion Photos, PetlinDmitry, NotionPic. 30 – BlackMac.

CONTENTS

PAGE 4 Ancient Rome
PAGE 6 The Empire's Emperors
PAGE 8 The Colosseum
PAGE 10 Gory Gladiators
PAGE 12 Health and Sickness
PAGE 14 Pretty Romans
PAGE 16 Squeaky Clean
PAGE 18 Roman Restrooms
PAGE 20 Washing with Wee
PAGE 22 Boys Did What?
PAGE 24 Girls Did What?
PAGE 26 Feasting Time
PAGE 28 Breaking the Law
PAGE 30 Your Place in History
PAGE 31 Glossary
PAGE 32 Index

Words that look like this are explained in the glossary on page 31.

ANCIENT ROME

Countless people have lived and died throughout history. In their time, some of them did some very odd things.

The ancient Romans started with the city of Rome. It was **founded** in 753 BCE. Ancient Rome lasted for over 1,000 years.

BCE means Before the Common Era. This is the time before the year 0.

Ancient Rome started as a small town. It grew much larger. First it was ruled by kings. Then, it was ruled as a **republic**. Then, it became an empire ruled by emperors.

At its biggest, the Roman Empire spread across parts of Europe, Asia and Africa. There were 65 million people living in the empire.

THE EMPIRE'S EMPERORS

The emperor was the most important person in the Roman Empire. There were some things that only the emperors were allowed to do.

The emperor was the only person in ancient Rome who could wear the colour purple. If anyone else wore purple clothes, they were punished. Some had to pay a fine, but others were killed for it.

Emperor Nero

Emperor Nero loved to sing, whether people liked it or not. He had 5,000 of his soldiers clap for him when he performed.

Emperors got away with acting very strangely because they were so powerful. People loved Emperor Tiberius at first. Then, he wanted everyone to treat him like a god. He also tried to make his horse a politician.

Emperor Tiberius

THE COLOSSEUM

Emperor Vespasian thought that the people of Rome needed some entertainment. So, he built a huge amphitheatre called the Colosseum. The Colosseum could fit 50,000 people. Some of it is still standing today.

Thousands of people went to see gladiator fights in the Colosseum. Gladiators fought each other or wild animals, such as tigers, lions, giraffes and rhinos.

The Colosseum held lots of different shows. Sometimes, the Colosseum was used for **executions**. Many of these executions involved forcing people to fight wild animals.

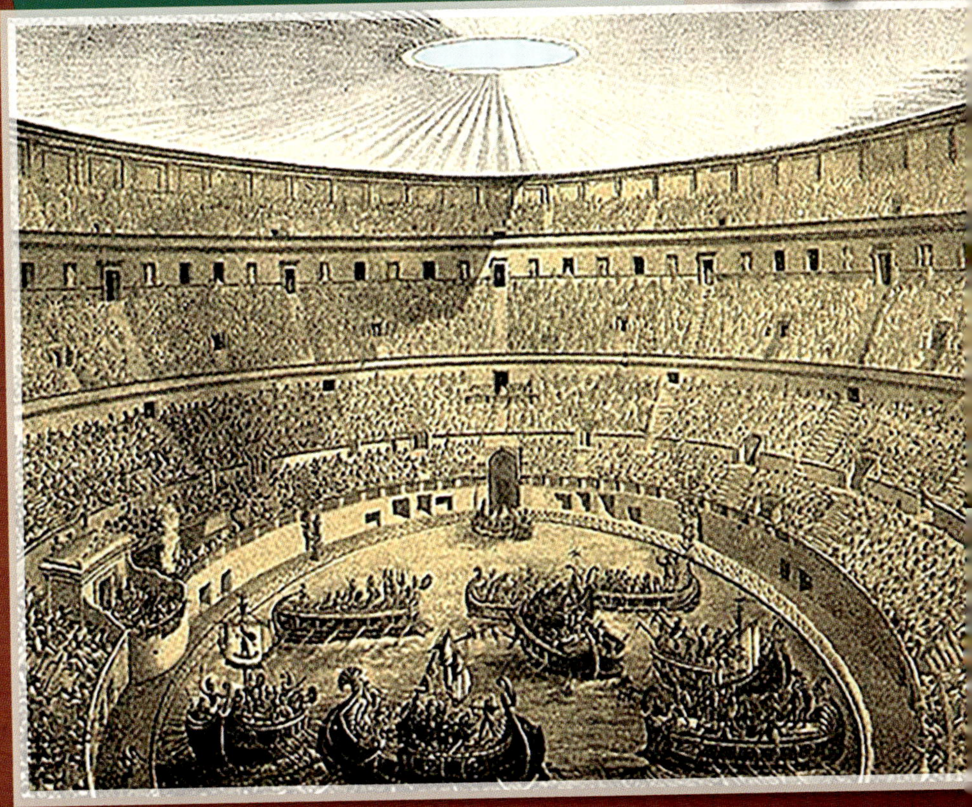

Naumachia shows were another strange kind of show. For these, the amphitheatre was flooded and ships sailed in the water. These ships then recreated famous sea battles for the audience.

GORY GLADIATORS

Many of the gladiators who fought in the Colosseum were slaves or prisoners. Sometimes, gladiators who won their battles and put on good shows became famous. A few Roman citizens trained to be gladiators because they wanted to be famous too.

There were different kinds of gladiators who used different weapons in their battles.

Thraex gladiators used curved swords. Their helmets covered their entire heads. They fought against the hoplomachus gladiators. Hoplomachus gladiators fought with spears and round shields.

Retiarius gladiators did not wear much armour. They used a net and a trident to fight secutor gladiators. Secutor gladiators had round helmets to stop them from getting caught in the retiarius gladiators' nets.

HEALTH AND SICKNESS

Ancient Romans had lots of strange ways to treat sick people.

DO NOT TRY THESE ANCIENT ROMAN TREATMENTS.

To get rid of warts, all you needed was to spread honey and burnt cow poo on your skin.

Are you struggling to poo? Just mix salt, milk, honey and wolf bile and put it in your belly button.

Jaundice is a health problem where the skin turns yellowish. The ancient Romans believed that donkey poo helped. They mixed the first poo of a baby donkey with wine and drank it.

The ancient Romans also thought that being touched by an elephant trunk would treat a headache. It was even better if the elephant sneezed on you.

PRETTY ROMANS

The ancient Romans cared a lot about looking pretty. They used dye to keep their hair looking nice. The hair dye they used was made from a mix of ashes, walnut shells and worms.

Sometimes, Romans had jewellery that was dipped in the blood of their favourite gladiator. They also used face cream that was made with gladiator sweat.

Many ancient Roman women wanted lighter skin. They put white chalk and lead on their faces to look pale. However, they did not know that lead was poisonous. It ended up doing a lot of damage to their health.

Some women also wanted to have dark eyebrows and eyelashes. They used the soot from fires to make these parts darker.

SQUEAKY CLEAN

Ancient Romans stayed clean by going to the public baths. The public baths were an important part of life. Romans could also exercise, meet friends and do business at public baths.

Aqueduct

Aqueducts were how Romans got water to their baths. Aqueducts were channels that water would flow down from lakes or springs. Some aqueducts stretched for many kilometres.

The caldarium was a room in the baths that had pools of hot water. Romans sat in the caldarium and got sweaty. Then, they used a metal tool called a strigil to scrape off all the dirt and dead skin.

Romans finished in the baths by going to the frigidarium. This room had cold water where they could cool down.

ROMAN RESTROOMS

Ancient Romans also had public toilets. Instead of cubicles, all of the toilets were next to each other. This let you chat to the person sat next to you.

After doing their business, ancient Romans cleaned up with a sponge on a stick. There was running water along the floor to give the sponge a clean, ready for the next person.

Public toilets were connected to underground sewers. These sewers became homes for some creatures. There was a risk that a rat or a snake might come out of your toilet.

There was another risk. All the gas in the sewers could build up and catch fire. Hopefully, you were not sat on the toilet when that happened!

WASHING WITH WEE

Romans liked to keep their clothes fresh and clean. However, they had a strange way of washing them.

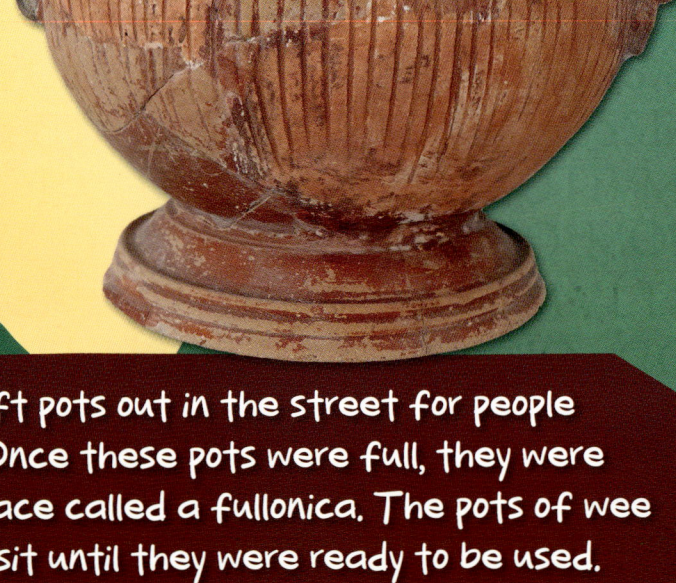

First, they left pots out in the street for people to wee into. Once these pots were full, they were taken to a place called a fullonica. The pots of wee were left to sit until they were ready to be used.

The pots of wee were poured into a big pit with clay and water. The dirty clothes were then thrown into this smelly mix. Someone called a fullo climbed into the pit and stamped on the clothes.

After that, they were rinsed with water and hung up to dry. Hopefully, the smell of wee came off them.

BOYS DID WHAT?

Boys went to school if their families were rich enough. If not, they stayed at home and worked with their parents.

1	I	11	XI	30	XXX
2	II	12	XII	40	XL
3	III	13	XIII	50	L
4	IV	14	XIV	60	LX
5	V	15	XV	70	LXX
6	VI	16	XVI	80	LXXX
7	VII	17	XVII	90	XC
8	VIII	18	XVIII	100	C
9	IX	19	XIX	500	D
10	X	20	XX	1000	M

Boys who went to school were taught how to read and write. Maths was also very important. Roman numbers were written as numerals. Numerals were letters that were used to represent numbers. They could get very confusing.

Schoolchildren used wax tablets instead of paper. Letters and numerals were carved into the wax. Then, fresh wax could be added so the tablet could be used again.

Schoolboys were followed by a slave called a paedagogus. The paedagogus made sure the boys behaved. If they did not, the naughty children could be punished.

GIRLS DID WHAT?

Girls did not go to school with the boys. Girls from rich families had tutors come to their houses to teach them. Girls from poor families worked with their parents.

Girls with tutors were taught maths and how to read and write. However, girls were mostly taught how to take care of the household.

Large homes in ancient Rome were called villas. Villas were home to families, as well as all of their servants. Materfamilias were the women in charge of the household.

Materfamilias taught their children. They also told all of the servants what to do. Materfamilias needed to be good at maths because they were in charge of the family's money.

FEASTING TIME

Rich Romans loved to have big feasts to show off to their guests. The richer the Roman, the fancier the feast.

Dormice were a very fancy treat to serve your guests. The dormice were kept alive in a pot called a glirarium. The dormice ate and slept in the glirarium all day to fatten them up for dinnertime.

An ancient Roman dining room was called a triclinium. The triclinium was decorated with paintings and mosaics. The Romans ate their meals while laid down on sofas.

A good Roman dinner party also had some entertainment. Most of the time, the entertainers would dance or play musical instruments. Some big feasts even had their own gladiator fights.

BREAKING THE LAW

Roman citizens had to follow the law. The Twelve Tables were a set of Roman laws that were written on bronze tablets. One law said that women could not cry at funerals. Another said that you could not have meetings at night.

Some citizens managed to avoid getting punished. However, others were not so lucky.

One punishment was to put the **criminal** into a sack with a monkey, a dog, a snake and a cockerel. The sack was tied up and thrown into the sea.

Women at a temple for the goddess Vesta had to make sure a fire stayed burning. If it went out, they were punished by being buried alive.

YOUR PLACE IN HISTORY

Could you live in ancient Rome? Would you wash your clothes with wee? Could you share a sponge with someone in the public toilets?

If ancient Roman life is too difficult for you, why not try another time in history? Just be warned! The ancient Romans are not the only ones who will leave you thinking...

What bizarre behaviour!

GLOSSARY

AMPHITHEATRE — an open, round theatre with layers of seats for spectators

BILE — a yellowy or dark-green fluid in the stomach which helps break down food

CARVED — cut into shape

CITIZENS — legally recognised members of a country

CRIMINAL — someone who has committed a crime or broken the law

EXECUTIONS — death sentences

FOUNDED — started something new

POLITICIAN — a person involved with politics and the government

REPRESENT — to stand for something else

REPUBLIC — a type of government where the people get to pick who leads them

SLAVES — people who are owned by another person and have no freedom

INDEX

aqueducts 16

baths 16—17

clothes 6, 20—21, 30

emperors 5—8

fires 15, 19, 29

gladiators 8, 10—11, 14, 27

hair 14

jewellery 14

numerals 22—23

sewers 19

sponges 18, 30